Audubon's
Art and Nature

Audubon's Art and Nature

A Collection of Nature Writings

Illustrated With the Art of

John James Audubon

Edited by John Borneman

WINGS BOOKS

New York / Avenel, New Jersey

Copyright © 1995 by National Audubon Society, Inc.
All rights reserved.

This 1995 edition is published by Wings Books,
distributed by Random House Value Publishing, Inc.,
40 Engelhard Avenue, Avenel, New Jersey 07001,
by arrangement with the National Audubon Society, Inc.

Random House
New York • Toronto • London • Sydney • Auckland

Printed and bound in the United States of America

Library of Congress Cataloging-in-Publication Data
Audubon's art and nature : a collection of nature writings
illustrated with the art of John James Audubon.
        p.   cm.
    ISBN 0-517-14778-5 (hardcover)
1. Nature—Literary collections.   I. Audubon, John James,
1785–1851.
    PN6071.N3A93   1995
    808.8'036—dc20   95-8895
                                        CIP

    8 7 6 5 4 3 2 1

National Audubon Society

Mission Statement

The mission of the NATIONAL AUDUBON SOCIETY is to conserve and restore natural ecosystems, focusing on birds and other wildlife for the benefit of humanity and the earth's biological diversity.

In the vanguard of the environmental movement, AUDUBON has 500,000 members, 14 regional and state offices, and an extensive chapter network in the United States and Latin America, plus a professional staff of scientists, lobbyists, lawyers, policy analysts, and educators.

Through our nationwide sanctuary system we manage 150,000 acres of critical wildlife habitat and unique natural areas for birds, wild animals, and rare plant life.

Our award-winning *Audubon* magazine, published six times a year and sent to all members, carries outstanding articles and color photography on wildlife and nature, and presents in-depth reports on critical environmental issues, as well as conservation news and commentary. We also publish *Field Notes*, a journal reporting on seasonal bird sightings continent-wide, and *Audubon Adventures*, a bimonthly children's newsletter reaching 600,000 students.

Our acclaimed *World of Audubon* television documentaries deal with a variety of environmental themes. NATIONAL AUDUBON SOCIETY also sponsors books and electronic programs on nature, plus travel programs to exotic places like Africa, Antarctica, Australia, Baja California, Galapagos Islands, Indonesia, and Patagonia.

For information about how you can become a member, please write or call:

NATIONAL AUDUBON SOCIETY
Membership Dept.
700 Broadway
New York, New York 10003
212-979-3000

The whole art of teaching is only the art of awaking the natural curiosity of young minds for the purpose of satisfying it afterwards.

—Anatole France, "The Crime of Sylvestre Bonnard"

I grow old learning something new every day.

—Solon, *Valerius Maximus: Book VIII*

*T*he very idea of a bird is a symbol and a suggestion to the poet. A bird seems to be at the top of the scale, so vehement and intense is his life—large brained, large lunged, hot, ecstatic, his frame charged with buoyancy and his heart with song. The beautiful vagabonds, endowed with every grace, masters of all climes, and knowing no bounds—how many human aspirations are realized in their free, holiday-lives—and how many suggestions to the poets in their flight and song!

Indeed, is not the bird the original type and teacher of the poet, and do not we demand of the human lark or thrush that he "shake out his carols" in the same free and spontaneous manner of his winged prototype?

—John Burroughs, *Birds and Poets*

Goshawk.
FALCO PALUMBARIUS Linn.
Adult Male & Young. 2.

Stanley-Hawk.
FALCO STANLEII. Aud.
Adult. 3.

Northern Goshawk [Goshawk]
Falconiformes Accipitridae *Accipiter gentilis*

Calling a Bird a Bird

I really think that it's terrific
We're in an age most scientific.
But when our words get too pedantic
Let's not forget to wax romantic.

When we describe a flower or bird
Ignore the biologic word.
The name of "robin" means much more to us
Than calling it *Turdus migra-tor-ious*.

—John Borneman, *Memories of J.B.*

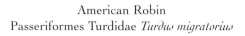

American Robin

Passeriformes Turdidae *Turdus migratorius*

Why Do Birds Sing

Let poets piece prismatic words,
Give me the jeweled joy of birds!

What ecstacy moves them to sing?
Is it the lyric glee of Spring,
The dewy rapture of the rose?
Is it the worship born in those
Who are of Nature's self a part,
The adoration of the heart?

Is it the mating mood in them
That makes each crystal note a gem?
Oh mocking bird and nightingale,
Oh mavis, lark and robin—hail!
Tell me what perfect passion glows
In your inspired arpeggios?

A thrush is thrilling as I write
Its obligato of delight;
And in its fervour, as in mine,
I fathom tenderness divine,
And pity those of earthy ear
Who cannot hear . . . who cannot hear.

Let poets pattern pretty words:
For lovely largess—bless you, Birds!

—Robert W. Service

Drawn from Nature by J.J. Audubon, F.R.S. F.L.S.   Engraved, Printed and Coloured by R Havell 1837

Townsend's Warbler.
SYLVIA TOWNSENDI, *Nuttall*
1. Male.

Arctic Blue-bird.
SIALIA ARCTICA, *Swain*
2. Male.   3. Female.
Plant { *Gaultheria Shallon*
          1. GAULTHERIA PRICEPS

Western Blue-bird.
SIALIA OCCIDENTALIS, *Townsend*
4. Male.   5. Female.

Townsend's Warbler	Mountain Bluebird	Western Bluebird
Passeriformes	[Arctic Blue Bird]	[Western Blue Bird]
Parulidae	Passeriformes Turdidae	Passeriformes Turdidae
Dendroica townsendi	*Sialia currucoides*	*Sialia mexicana*

Birds and Their Friends

Few who have not entered upon this study [birds] can imagine the pleasure to be found in it. Much can be learned from mere observation. To wander at will, in field and wood, with the ear open to catch any note or song of bird, and the eye trained to notice the least flutter in the branches, cannot fail to result in an interesting knowledge of bird-life. Every student should possess an opera glass. It is an efficient aid to the eye, and will often enable one to recognize a bird, when otherwise there might be much difficulty in its identification. The habits of birds are also much more readily watched without alarming any shy inhabitant of the wood, or interfering with the maternal cares of the more domestic species.

—Graceanna Lewis

Yellow-breasted Chat, ICTERIA VIRIDIS, _Male, Female, Sweet Briar, Rosa rubiginosa._

Yellow-breasted Chat
Passeriformes Parulidae *Icteria virens*

A Few of the Bird-Family

The Old Bob-white, and Chipbird;
The Flicker and the Chewink,
And little hopty-skip bird
Along the river-brink.

The Blackbird, and the Snowbird,
The Chicken-hawk, and Crane;
The glossy old black Crow-bird,
And Buzzard down the lane.

The Yellowbird, and Redbird,
The Tomtit, and the Cat;
The Thrush, and that Red*head*-bird
The rest's all pickin' at!

The Jay-bird, and the Bluebird,
The Sapsuck, and the Wren—
The Cockadoodle-doo-bird,
And our old Settin' hen!

—James Whitcomb Riley

PLATE. CCCV.

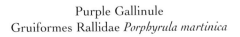

Drawn from Nature by J. J. Audubon, F.R.S. F.L.S.

Engraved, Printed & Coloured, by R. Havell, 1836.

Purple Gallinule.
GALLINULA MARTINICA. (Gmel)
Adult Male spring plumage.

Purple Gallinule
Gruiformes Rallidae *Porphyrula martinica*

I sometimes think the more I limit myself to a small area, the more novelties and discoveries I make in natural history. My observations for the past four summers have been almost wholly confined to an acre of ground in the heart of a noisy town. A bit of natural woodland occupies about a quarter of an acre, and here I made several discoveries new to science.

The most interesting creatures that have rewarded me in my search are two species of large burrowing spiders that had heretofore escaped the attention of naturalists. These spiders build beautiful complicated structures above their burrows, with which they take as much pains as most birds do in building their nests.

—Mary Treat, *Home Studies in Nature*

Band-tailed Pigeon 1. Male 2. Female
COLUMBA FASCIATA, Say.

Band-tailed Pigeon
Columbiformes Columbidae *Columba fasciata*

Sonnet to Solitude

O SOLITUDE! if I must with thee dwell,
Let it not be among the jumbled heap
Of murky buildings: climb with me the steep, —
Nature's observatory, —Whence the dell,
In flowery slopes, its river's crystal swell,
May seem a span; let me thy vigils keep
'Mongst boughs pavilion'd, where the
deer's swift leap
Startles the wild bee from the foxglove bell.

—John Keats

Yellow-throated Vireo.
VIREO FLAVIFRONS, Vieill.
Male.
Swamp Snowball. Hydrangea quercifolia.

Yellow-throated Vireo
Passeriformes Vireonidae *Vireo flavifrons*

When leading a group of sightless students on a field trip, we paused underneath a large sycamore tree. One of the boys asked: "What is this tree with the big leaves?"

"How do you know it has big leaves?" I asked.

"Because of the sound the leaves make as the wind blows through them," he said.

I thought how wonderful it would be if our senses were so attuned to the natural world that we would know:

The trees by their wind sounds,

The wildflowers by their scent,

The birds by their calls,

The insects by their raspings and dronings.

—John Borneman, *Memories of J. B.*

PLATE CXII

Downy Woodpecker.
PICUS PUBESCENS.

Male & Female.

Prognoma confoedata.

Downy Woodpecker
Piciformes Picidae *Picoides pubescens*

When Lilacs Last in the Dooryard Bloom'd

Sing on, sing on, you gray-brown bird,
Sing from the swamps and the recesses,
pour your chant from the bushes,
Limitless out of the dusk, out of the cedars and pines,
Sing on, dearest brother, warble your reedy song,
Loud human song, with voice of uttermost woe.
O liquid and free and tender!
O wild and loose to my soul—O wondrous singer!
You only I hear—yet the star holds me (but will soon depart),
Yet the lilac with mastering odor holds me.

—Walt Whitman

PLATE CCCVI

Great Northern Diver or Loon.
COLYMBUS GLACIALIS, *L.*
Adult 1. Young in Winter 2.

Common Loon [Great Northern Diver]
Gaviiformes Gaviidae *Gavia immer*

Spring Quiet

Gone were but the Winter,
Come were but the Spring,
I would go to a covert
Where the birds sing;

Where in the whitethorn
Singeth the thrush,
And a robin sings
In a holly-bush.

Full of fresh scents
Are the budding boughs
Arching high over
A cool green house;

Full of sweet scents,
And whispering air
Which sayeth softly:
"We spread no snare;

"Here dwell in safety,
Here dwell alone,
With a clear stream
And a mossy stone.

"Here the sun shineth
Most shadily;
Here is heard an echo
Of the far sea,
Though far off it be."

—Christina Rossetti

Roseate Spoonbill

Roseate Spoonbill
Ciconiiformes Threskiornithidae *Ajaia ajaja*

What a noble gift to man are the forests! What a debt of gratitude and admiration we owe to their utility and their beauty!

How pleasantly the shadows of the wood fall upon our heads, when we turn from the glitter and the turmoil of man!

The winds of heaven seem to linger amid these balmy branches, and the sunshine falls like a blessing upon the green leaves; the wild breath of the forest, fragrant with bark and berry, fans the brow with grateful freshness; and the beautiful wood-light, neither garish nor gloomy, full of calm and peaceful influences, sheds repose over the Spirit.

—Susan Fenimore Cooper, *Rural Hours*

Drawn from Nature by J.J. Audubon. F.R.S. F.L.S.

Snowy Heron, or White Egret.
ARDEA CANDIDISSIMA, Gm.
Male adult Spring plumage.
Rice Plantation – South Carolina.

Engraved, Printed, & coloured, by R. Havell, London 1835.

Snowy Egret [Snowy Heron]
Ciconiiformes Adeidae *Egretta thula*

I Stood Tiptoe Upon a Little Hill

Linger awhile upon some bending planks
That lean against a streamlet's rushing banks,
And watch intently Nature's gentle doings:
They will be found softer than a Ring-Doves cooings.
How silent comes the water round that bend;
Not the minutest whisper does it send
To the o'erhanging sallows: blades of grass
Slowly across the chequer'd shadows pass.
Why, you might read two sonnets, ere they reach
To where the the hurrying freshness aye preach
A natural sermon o'er their pebbly beds;
Where swarms of minnows show their little heads,
Staying their wavy bodies 'gainst the streams,
To taste the luxury of sunny beams
Temper'd with coolness. How they ever wrestle
With their own sweet delight, and ever nestle
Their silver bellies on the pebbly sand.

—John Keats

Carolina Turtle Dove, COLUMBA CAROLINENSIS, Male & Female? White flowered Stuartia. Stuartia malacodendron.

Mourning Dove [Canadian Turtle Dove or Carolina Pigeon]
Columbiformes Columbidae *Zenaida macroura*

Overheard in an Orchard

Said the robin to the sparrow,
"I should really like to know
Why these anxious human beings
Rush about and worry so."
Said the sparrow to the robin,
"Friend, I think that it must be
That they have no Heavenly Father
Such as cares for you and me."

—Elizabeth Cheney

White-crowned Sparrow
FRINGILLA LEUCOPHRYS,
Male 1.Female 2.
Simens Grape Vitis V. sidicalis.

White-crowned Sparrow
Passeriformes Emberizidae *Zonotrichia leucophrys*

*K*now you what it is to be a child? It is to be something very different from the man of today. It is to have a spirit yet streaming from waters of baptism; it is to believe in love, to believe in loveliness, to believe in belief; it is to be so little that elves can reach to whisper in your ears; it is to turn pumpkins into coaches, and mice into horses, lowness into loftiness, and nothing into everything, for each child has its fairy godmother in its own soul; it is to live in a nutshell and to count yourself the king of infinite space; it is

> To see a world in a grain of sand,
> And a heaven in a wildflower,
> Hold infinity in the palm of your hand,
> And eternity in an hour;

When we become conscious in the dreaming that we dream, the dream is on the point of breaking; when we become conscious in living that we live, the ill dream is but just beginning.

—Francis Thompson, *Shelley*

PLATE CXVI

Willow Grous
TETRAO SALICETI, *Swain.*
Male 1 Female 2 & Young.
Labrador. Sect 5 Aug from ?

Willow Ptarmigan [Willow Grous or Large Ptarmigan]
Galliformes Phasianidae *Lagopus lagopus*

The Old Oaken Bucket

How dear to my heart are the scenes of my childhood,
When fond recollection presents them to view!
The orchard, the meadow, the deep tangled wildwood,
And every loved spot that my infancy knew,
The wide-spreading pond and the mill that stood by it,
The bridge and the rock where the cataract fell;
The cot of my father, the dairy house nigh it,
And e'en the rude bucket that hung in the well.

—Samuel Woodworth

House Wren
TROGLODYTES AEDON Wils.
Male 1, female 2, Young 3, & 3.

Drawn from Nature and Published by John J. Audubon, F.R.S. F.L.S.

Engraved, Printed & Coloured by R. Havell.

House Wren
Passeriformes Troglodytidae *Troglodytes aedon*

Loveliest of Trees, the Cherry Now

Loveliest of trees, the cherry now
Is hung with blooms along the bough,
And stands along the woodland ride
Wearing white for Eastertide.

Now, of my threescore years and ten,
Twenty will not come again,
And take from seventy springs a score,
It only leaves me fifty more.

And since to look at things in bloom
Fifty springs are little room,
About the woodlands I will go
To see the cherry hung with snow.

—A. E. Housman

Piriy Flycatcher
MUSCICAPA DOMINICENSIS.
Acacia grandiflora

Gray Kingbird [Gray Tyrant]
Passeriformes Tyrannidae *Tyrannus dominicensis*

My November Guest

My sorrow, when she's here with me,
Thinks these dark days of autumn rain
Are beautiful as days can be;
She loves the bare, the withered tree;
She walks the sodden pasture lane.

Her pleasure will not let me stay.
She talks and I am fain to list:
She's glad the birds are gone away,
She's glad her simple worsted grey
Is silver now with clinging mist.

The desolate, deserted trees,
The faded earth, the heavy sky,
The beauties she so truly sees,
She thinks I have no eye for these,
And vexes me for reason why.

Not yesterday I learned to know
The love of bare November days
Before the coming of the snow;
But it were vain to tell her so,
And they are better for her praise.

—Robert Frost

Drawn from Nature by J.J.Audubon, F.R.S. F.L.S.　　　　　　　　　Engraved, Printed and Coloured by R.Havell 1837.

Pine Grosbeak.
PYRRHULA ENUCLEATOR.
Male Adult. Spring Plumage 1. Female 2. Young near Winter 3.

Pine Grosbeak
Passeriformes Fringillidae *Pinicola enucleator*

Fable

The mountain and the squirrel
Had a quarrel;
And the former called the latter "Little Prig."
Bun replied,
"You are doubtless very big;
But all sorts of things and weather
Must be taken in together
To make up a year
And a sphere.

And I think it's no disgrace
To occupy my place.
If I'm not so large as you,
You are not so small as I,
And not half so spry.
I'll not deny you make
A very pretty squirrel track;
Talents differ: all is well and wisely put;
If I cannot carry forests on my back,
Neither can you crack a nut."

—Ralph Waldo Emerson

Raven.
CORVUS CORAX.
Male.

Common Raven [Raven]
Passeriformes Corvidae *Corvus corax*

Bird Names and Bird Brains

I f you were out with a bunch of ornithologists and said, "Look at the yellow-shafted flicker!" you would be corrected. "That is now called the northern flicker," they would respond contemptuously. But, don't dispair, for the bird cares not what you call it. In 1917 it was called: yellow-shafted woodpecker; golden-winged woodpecker; clape; pigeon woodpecker; yellow-hammer; high-hole; high-holder; yarrup; wake-up; wood-pigeon; high-ho; wick-up; hairy wicket; yawker bird; walk-up! A researcher, who thought he had exhausted all of the names of the flicker, asked a plantation worker the name of this woodpecker as it flew by in its undulating flight. "A wup-d'-wup" he replied. "Why do you call it that?" asked the scholar. "Because of the way it flies: wup—d'-wup-d'-wup," he said as he imitated its flight with his outstretched hand.*

—John Borneman, *Memories of J.B.*

*A true story related to me by the late Ira Gabrielson of the World Wildlife Fund

Hairy Woodpecker
Piciformes Picidae *Picoides villosus*

My Early Home

Here sparrows built upon the trees,
And stock-dove hides her nest;
The leaves are winnowed by the breeze
Into a calmer rest:
The blackcap's song was very sweet,
That used the rose to kiss;
It made the paradise complete:
My early home was this.

The redbreast from the sweetbrier bush
Dropt down to pick the worm;
On the horse-chestnut sang the thrush,
O'er the house where I was born;
The moonlight like a shower of pearls,
Fell o'er this "bower of bliss,"
And on the bench sat boys and girls:
My early home was this.

The old house stooped just like a cave,
Thatched o'er with mosses green;
Winter around the walls would rave,
But all was calm within;
The trees are here all green agen,
Here bees the flowers still kiss,
But flowers and trees seemed sweeter then:
My early home was this.

—John Clare

Field Sparrow FRINGILLA PUSILLA, Wils.
Male. *Calopogon pulchellum.* & *Vaccinium tenellum.*

Drawn from Nature by J.J.Audubon F.R.S.F.L.S.   Engraved, Printed & Coloured by R. Havell London.

Field Sparrow
Passeriformes Emberizidae *Spizella pusilla*

. . . He prayeth well who loveth well
Both man and bird and beast.

He prayeth best who loveth best
All things both great and small;
For the dear God who loveth us,
He made and loveth all.

—Samuel Taylor Coleridge, *The Ancient Mariner*

PLATE CCCXIV.

Drawn from Nature by J. J. Audubon, F.R.S. F.L.S.

Engraved, Printed & Coloured by R. Havell, 1836.

Black-headed Gull.
LARUS ATRICILLA. *L.*
Adult Male Spring Plumage 1 Young first Autumn 2.

Laughing Gull [Black-headed Gull]
Charadriiformes Laridae *Larus atricilla*

The Deserted Garden

I mind me in the days departed,
How often underneath the sun
With childish bounds I used to
    run
      To a garden long deserted.

The beds and walks were
    vanished quite;
And whereso'er had struck the
    spade,
The greenest grasses Nature laid
    To sanctify her right.

Adventurous joy it was for me!
I crept beneath the boughs and
    found
A circle smooth of mossy ground
    Beneath a poplar-tree.

Old garden rose-trees hedged
    it in,
Bedropt with roses white,

Well satisfied with dew and light,
    And careless to be seen.

To me upon my mossy seat,
Though never a dream the roses
    sent
Of science or love's compliment,
    I ween they smelt as sweet.

And gladdest hours for me did
    glide
In silence at the rose-tree wall,
A thrush made gladness musical
    Upon the other side.

Nor he nor I did e'er incline
To peck or pluck the blossoms
    white.
How should I know that roses
    might
    Lead lives as glad as mine?

—Elizabeth Barrett Browning

Sea-side Finch.
FRINGILLA MARITIMA, *&c. 2? Wank Carolina Rose.— Rosa carolina.*

Seaside Sparrow [Sea-side Finch]
Passeriformes Emberizidae *Ammodramus maritimus*

The Pass in September

I was driving over the Northern California Coast Range at night. There was no moon and the surrounding, oak-covered pass was alive with the whirring sounds of insect life. The sounds would amplify and diminish as I rounded curves in the road that took me from slope to draw and back again. When I reached the top of the pass, I pulled over to the side of the road, shut the engine off and got out of the car. The night was as black as a night can get and I found myself in the vortex of a maelstrom of high-pitched, sustained sizzling of hundreds of thousands of night-singing insects. I didn't know if they were cicadas or leaf-hoppers. What I did know was that I was conscious of the fact that there was an urgency in their singing: It was time to get the mating and egg laying accomplished before the cold, autumn rains arrived.

—John Borneman, *Memories of J. B.*

PLATE CCCCXXIX

Drawn from Nature by J. J. Audubon, F.R.S. F.L.S.

Engraved, Printed and Coloured by Rob.t Havell. 1836.

Western Duck
FULIGULA STELLERI, *Bonap.*

Steller's Eider [Western Duck]
Anseriformes Anatidae *Polysticta stelleri*

The Poet

*T*he poet alone knows astronomy, chemistry, vegetation and animation, for he does not stop at these facts, but employs them as signs. He knows why the plain or meadow of space was strown with these flowers we call suns, and moons, and stars; why the great deep is adorned with animals, with men and gods; for, in every word he speaks he rides on them as horses of thought.

By virtue of this science the poet is the Namer, or Language-maker, naming things sometimes after their appearance, sometimes after their essence, and giving to every one its own name and not another's, thereby rejoicing the intellect, which delights in detachment or boundary. The poets made all the words, and therefore language is the archives of history, and, if we must say it, a sort of tomb of the muses. For, though the origin of most of our words is forgotten, each word was at first a stroke of genius, and obtained currency, because for the moment it symbolized the world to the first speaker and to the hearer.

—Ralph Waldo Emerson, *Essays*

PLATE CCLIX

Drawn from Nature by J.J.Audubon. F.R.S. F.L.

Engraved, Printed, & Coloured by R.Havell 1835.

Horned Grebe.
PODICEPS CORNUTUS, Lath.
Adult Male, 1. Female Winter plumage 2.

Horned Grebe
Podicipediformes Podicipedidae *Podiceps auritus*

October's Bright Blue Weather

O suns and skies and clouds of
   June,
And flowers of June together,
Ye cannot rival for one hour
October's bright blue weather.

When loud the humblebee makes
   haste,
Belated, thriftless vagrant,
And Golden Rod is dying fast,
And lanes with grapes are
   fragrant;

When Gentians roll their fringes
   tight,
To save them for the morning,
And chestnuts fall from satin
   burrs
Without a sound or warning;

When on the ground red apples
   lie,
In piles like jewels shining,
And redder still on old stone
   walls
Are leaves of woodbine twining;

When all the lovely wayside
   things
Their white-winged seeds are
   sowing,
And in the fields, still green and
   fair,
Late aftermaths are growing;

When springs run low, and on
   the brooks,
In idle golden freighting,
Bright leaves sink noiseless in the
   hush
Of woods, for winter waiting;

When comrades seek sweet
   country haunts,
By twos and twos together,
And count like misers, hour by
   hour,
October's bright blue weather.

O suns and skies and flowers of
   June,
Count all your boasts together,
  Love loveth best of all the year
  October's bright blue weather.

—Helen Hunt Jackson

Yellow rump Warbler.
SYLVIA CORONATA Lath.
Male / Young 2
Vine (vironcle).

Drawn from Nature by J.J.Audubon FRS FLS.
Engraved, Printed & Coloured by R.Havell, London 1837.

Yellow-rumped Warbler [Yellow-crown Warbler]
Passseriformes Parulidae *Dendroica coronata*

To sit and hear and see and feel
When I am out-of-doors,
And close my mind to thoughts of crime,
Of pestilence and wars:
This is an exercise that helps
To nourish heart and soul,
And strengthen me to carry on
To reach some earthly goal.

—John Borneman, *Memories of J.B.*

Drawn from Nature by J.J. Audubon. F.R.S. F.L.S.   Engraved, Printed & Coloured by R. Havell.London.1835.

Cayenne Tern.
STERNA CAYANA, Lath.
Male Adult. Spring plumage.

Royal Tern [Cayenne Tern]
Charadriiformes Laridae *Sterna maxima*

$\mathscr{F}$inally, beloved, whatever is true, whatever is honorable, whatever is just, whatever is pleasing, whatever is commendable, if there is anything worthy of praise, think about these things. Keep on doing the things that you have learned and received and heard and seen in me, and the God of peace will be with you.

— Philippians 4:8, 9

Mango Humming Bird.

TROCHILUS MANGO.

Males 1, 2, 3. Females 4, 5.

Bignonia grandiflora.

Drawn from Nature by J.J.Audubon, F.R.S. F.L.S

Engraved, Printed & Coloured by R. Havell, 1833.

Black-throated Mango [Mangrove Humming Bird]
Apodiformes Trochilidae *Anthracothorax nigricollis*

The Grasshopper and the Cricket

The poetry of earth is never dead;
When all the birds are faint with the hot sun
And hide in cooling trees, a voice will run
From hedge to hedge about the new-mown mead.
That is the grasshopper's—he takes the lead
In summer luxury—he has never done
With his delights; for, when tired out with fun,
He rests at ease beneath some pleasant weed.
The poetry of earth is ceasing never.
On a lone winter evening, when the frost
Has wrought a silence, from the stove there shrills
The cricket's song, in warmth increasing ever,
And seems, to one in drowsiness half lost,
The grasshopper's among some grassy hills.

—John Keats

Cardinal Grosbeak.

FRINGILLA CARDINALIS - Bonap

Male 1 Female 2
Wild Almond

Drawn from Nature by J.J. Audubon, F.R.S. F.L.S.   Engraved, Printed & Coloured by R.Havell, London, 1827

Northern Cardinal [Cardinal Grosbeak]
Passeriformes Carlinalidae *Cardinalis cardinalis*

When the first baby laughed for the first time,
the laugh broke into a thousand pieces
and they all went skipping about,
and that was the beginning of fairies.

—James M. Barrie, *Peter Pan,* Act 1

Golden-Eye Duck?
FULIGULA CLANGULA.
Male & Female

Barrow's Goldeneye [Golden-eye Duck]
Anseriformes Anatidae *Bucephala islandica*

April 22, 1871. But such a lovely damasking in the sky as today I never felt before. The blue was charged with simple instress, the higher, zenith sky earnest and frowning, lower more light and sweet. High up again, breathing through woolly coats of cloud or on the quains and branches of the flying pieces it was the true exchange of crimson, nearer the earth . . . against the sun . . . it was turquoise, and in the opposite south-western bay below the sun it was like clear oil but just as full of color, shaken over with slanted flashing "traveler," all in flight, stepping one behind the other, their edges tossed with bright ravelling, as if white napkins were thrown up in the sun but not quite at the same moment so that they were all in a scale down the air falling one after the other to the ground.

—Gerard Manley Hopkins, *The Journal*

Black-bellied Darter
PLOTUS ANHINGA, *L.*

Anhinga [Black-bellied Darter]
Pelecaniformes Anhingidae *Anhinga anhinga*

The Rhodora

Lines On Being Asked, Whence Is the Flower

In May, when sea-winds pierced our solitudes,
I found the fresh Rhodora in the woods,
Spreading its leafless blooms in a damp nook,
To please the desert and the sluggish brook.
The purple petals, fallen in the pool,
Made the black water with their beauty gay;
Here might the red-bird come his plumes to cool,
And court the flower that cheapens his array.
Rhodora! if sages ask thee why
This charm is wasted on the earth and sky,
Tell them, dear, that if eyes were made for seeing,
Then Beauty is its own excuse for being:
Why thou wert there, O rival of the rose!
I never thought to ask, I never knew;
But, in my simple ignorance, suppose
The self-same Power that brought me there brought you.

—Ralph Waldo Emerson

Columbian Humming Bird.
TROCHILUS ANNA, *Lesson*
1, 2, 3, Males. 4, Female and Nest.
Plant, Ribesium Virginianum.

Drawn from Nature by J. J. Audubon, F.R.S. F.L.S.

Engraved, Printed and Coloured by R. Havell, 1839.

Anna's Hummingbird [Columbian Humming Bird]
Apodiformes Trochilidae *Calypte anna*

Care is no cure, but rather corrosive,
For things that are not to be remedied.

—William Shakespeare, *King Henry VI*, Part I, Act 3

PLATE CCCCVII

Dusky Albatros
DIOMEDEA FUSCA.

Sooty Albatross [Dusky Albatross]
Procellariiformes Diomedeidae *Phoebetria fusca*

Winter Song

Summer joys are o'er;
Flowerets bloom no more,
Wintry winds are sweeping;
Through the snow-drifts peeping,
Cheerful evergreen
Rarely now is seen.

Now no pluméd throng
Charms the wood with song;
Ice-bound trees are glittering;
Merry snow-birds, twittering,
Fondly strive to cheer
Scenes so cold and drear.

Winter, still I see
Many charms in thee, —
Love thy chilly greeting,
Snow-storms fiercely beating,
And the dear delights
Of the long, long nights.

—Ludwig Hölty

Translated from the German by Charles T. Brooks

Iceland or Jer Falcon.
FALCO ISLANDICUS. Lath.

Gryfalcon [Iceland or Jer Falcon]
Falconiformes Falconidae *Falco rusticolus*

Beneath the crisp and wintry carpet hid
A million buds but stay their blossoming;
And trustful birds have built ther nests amid
The shuddering boughs, and only wait to sing
Till one soft shower from the south shall bid,
And hither tempt the pilgrim steps of Spring.

—Robert Bridges, *The Growth of Love*, Sonnet 6

Chestnut-backed Titmouse 1 Male 2 Female
PARUS RUFESCENS, Townsend

Black-capt Titmouse 3 Male 4 Female
PARUS ATRICAPILLUS, Wils.

Chestnut-crowned Titmouse 5 Male 6 Female
PARUS MINIMUS, Townsend

| Chestnut-backed Chickadee [Chestnut-backed Titmouse] Passeriformes Paridae *Parus rufescens* | Black-capped Chickadee [Black-capt Titmouse] Passeriformes Paridae *Parus atricapillus* | Bushtit [Chestnut-crowned Titmouse] Passeriformes Aegithalide *Psaltriparus minimus* |

he humble moss beneath our feet, the sweet flowers, the varied shrubs, the great trees, and the sky gleaming above in sacred blue, are each the handiwork of God.

—Susan Fenimore Cooper, *Rural Hours*

PLATE CCXXXII.

Hooded Merganser. MERGUS CUCULLATUS. 1. Male. 2. Female.

Hooded Merganser
Anseriformes Anatidae *Lophodytes cucullatus*

To A Waterfowl

Whither, midst falling dew,
While glow the heavens with the last steps of day,
Far, through their rosy depths, dost thou pursue
Thy solitary way?

Vainly the fowler's eye
Might mark thy distant flight to do thee wrong,
As, darkly seen against the crimson sky,
Thy figure floats along.

Seek'st thou the plashy brink
Of weedy lake, or marge of river wide,
Or where the rocking billows rise and sink
On the chafed ocean-side?

There is a Power whose care
Teaches thy way along the pathless coast —
The desert and illimitable air —
Lone wandering, but not lost. And soon that toil shall end;
Soon shalt thou find a summer home, and rest,

And scream among thy fellows; reeds shall bend,
Soon, o'er thy sheltered nest.

— William Cullen Bryant

Goosander.
MERGUS MERGANSER, L
Male & Female, 2

Common Merganser [Goosander]
Anseriformes Anatidae *Mergus merganser*

Winter Animals

What is a country without rabbits and partridges? They are among the most simple animal products; ancient and venerable families known to antiquity as to modern times; of the very hue and substance of Nature, nearest allied to leaves and to ground—and to one another; it is either winged or it is legged. It is hardly as if you had seen a wild creature when a rabbit or a partridge bursts away, only a natural one, as much to be expected as rustling leaves. The partridge and the rabbit are still sure to thrive, like true natives of the soil, whatever revolutions occur. If the forest is cut off, the sprouts and bushes which spring up afford them concealment, and they become more numerous than ever. That must be a poor country indeed that does not support a hare. Our woods teem with them both, and around every swamp may be seen the partridge or rabbit walk.

—Henry David Thoreau, *Walden*

But for me the heart of California lies in the Condor country. And for me the heart of mystery, of wonder, and of desire lies with the Californa Condor, that majestic and almost legendary figure, which still haunts the fastness of our lessening wilderness.

—William Leon Dawson, *The Birds of California*, Volume 3

PLATE CCCCXIII

Drawn from Nature by J. J. Audubon F.R.S. F.L.S.

Californian Partridae
PERDIX CALIFORNICA, *Lath*.
Male 1. Female 2

Engraved, Printed, and Coloured by Rob.ᵗ Havell. 1838.

California Quail [Californian Partridge]
Galliformes Phasianidae *Callipepla californicus*

In the Quiet Night

So bright a gleam on the foot of my bed—
Could there have been a frost already?
Lifting myself to look, I found that it was moonlight.
Sinking back again, I thought suddenly of home.

—Li Po (A.D. 701–762)

Look at the stars! look, look up at the skies!
O look at all the fire-folk sitting in the air!

—Gerard Manley Hopkins, "The Starlight Night"

American White Pelican
Pelecaniformes Pelecanidae *Pelecanus erythorhynchos*

Indian Summer

From gold to gray
Our mild sweet day
Of Indian summer fades too soon;
But tenderly
Above the sea
Hangs, white and calm, the hunter's moon.

In its pale fire,
The village spire
Shows like the zodiac's Spectral lance;
The painted walls
Whereon it falls
Transfigured stand in marble trance!

—John Greenleaf Whittier

PLATE CCCCIX

Drawn from Nature by J.J.Audubon F.R.S. F.L.S.

Engraved, Printed and Coloured by Rob.t Havell. 1835

Havell's Tern ♀ 1
STERNA HAVELLI, *Aud.*

Trudeau's Tern ♀ 2
STERNA TRUDEAUI, *Aud.*

Forster's Tern [Havell's Tern]
Charadriiformes Laridae *Sterna forsteri*

In Springtime

All Nature seems at work—slugs leave their lair,
The bees are stirring—birds are on the wing,
And winter, slumbering in the open air,
Wears on his smiling face a dream of spring;
And I, the while, the sole unbusy thing,
Nor honey make, nor pair, nor build, nor sing.

—Samuel Taylor Coleridge

Cedar Bird.

BOMBYCILLA CAROLINENSIS, Brib.
Male 1 Female 2.
Red Cedar. Juniperus virginiana.

Cedar Waxwing [Cedar Bird]
Passeriformes Bombycillidae *Bombycilla cedrorum*

Aug. 30, 1867. Fair; in afternoon fine; the clouds had a good deal of crisping and mottling. . . . Putting my hand up against the sky whilst we lay on the grass I saw more richness and beauty in the blue than I had known before, not brilliance but glow and color. It was not transparent and sapphire-like, but turquoise-like, swarming and blushing round the edge of the hand and in pieces clipped in by fingers, the flesh being sometimes sunlit, sometimes glassy with reflected light, sometimes lightly shadowed in that violet one makes with cobalt and Indian red.

—Gerard Manley Hopkins, *The Journal*

Scarlet Ibis.
1013 RUBRA, Vieill
1. Adult Male. 2. Female. Second Summer.

Scarlet Ibis
Ciconiiformes Threskiornithidae *Eudocimus ruber*

A Song of Joy

. . . O gleesome saunter over fields and hillsides!
The leaves and flowers of the commonest weeds, the moist, fresh stillness
   of the woods,
The exquisite smell of the earth at daybreak, and all throughout the
   forenoon.

—Walt Whitman

The greatest lessons of Nature through the universe are perhaps
the lessons of variety and freedom.

—Walt Whitman, "Democratic Vistas"

PLATE CCCXVII

Black or Surf Duck

Surf Scoter [Surf Duck]
Anseriformes Anatidae *Melanitta perspicillata*

*I*t is springtime in Tucson. A golden mist of blossoms veils the pale green of the palo-verde trees; balls of yellow down gleam among the feathery leaves of mesquite and cat's-claw; torches of flame-colored flowers sway on the ends of the slender branches of ocatillo [sic], and the desert floor is spread with a carpet of many hues among which golden-hearted cactus blossoms reflect the sunlight from silken petals of pale yellow, pink, burnt-orange and deep crimson.

—Edith Clements, *Ecology and World War I*

I defy any intelligent human being to mix up for thirty days with the abounding cacti of the finest region of the South-west without becoming keenly interested in them. In one way or another, each species will impress itself upon the traveller, until at last he feels a proprietary interest in them all.

—William T. Hornaday, *Campfires on Desert and Lava*, 1909

Grass Finch or Bay-winged Bunting.
FRINGILLA GRAMINEA, *Gmel.*
Male.
Prickly Pear or Indian Fig, Cactus Opuntia.

Drawn from Nature, and Published by John J. Audubon, F.R.S.F.L.S.   Engraved, Printed & Coloured by R. Havell

Vesper Sparrow [Bay-winged Bunting]
Passeriformes Emberizidae *Pooecetes gramineus*

The Spell of the Yukon

... The summer—no sweeter was ever;
The sunshiny woods all athrill;
The grayling aleap in the river,
The bighorn asleep on the hill.
The strong life that never knows harness;
The wilds where the caribou call;
The freshness, the freedom, the farness—
O God! how I'm stuck on it all.

—Robert W. Service

Florida Jay

CORVUS FLORIDANUS. (Bonap.)

Male. Female. ♀

Persea Tree. *Persÿa carolinensis.*

Scrub Jay [Florida Jay]
Passeriformes Corvidae *Aphelocoma coerulescens*

Woodnotes

Many haps fall in the field
Seldom seen by wishful eyes,
But all her shows did Nature yield,
to please and win this pilgrim wise.
He saw the partridge drum in the woods;
He heard the woodcock's evening hymn;
He found the tawny thrushes' broods;
And the shy hawk did wait for him;
What others did at distance hear,
And guessed within the thicket's gloom,
Was shown to this philosopher,
And at his bidding seemed to come.

—Ralph Waldo Emerson

Broad-winged Hawk

Falconiformes Accipitridae *Buteo platypterus*

What is the pill that will keep us well, serene, contented? Not my or thy great-grandfather's, but our great-grandmother Nature's universal, vegetable, botanic medicines, by which she has kept herself young always, outlived so many old Parrs in her day, and fed her health with their decaying fatness. For my panacea, instead of one of those quack vials of a mixture dipped from Acheron and the Dead Sea, which come out of those long shallow black-schooner looking wagons which we sometimes see made to carry bottles, let me have a draught of undiluted morning air. Morning air! If men will not drink of this at the fountain-head of the day, why, then, we must even bottle up some and sell it in the shops, for the benefit of those who have lost their subscription ticket to morning time in this world. But remember, it will not keep quite till noonday even in the coolest cellar, but drive out the stopples long ere that and follow westward the steps of Aurora.

— Henry David Thoreau, *Walden*

Little Blue Heron [Blue Crane or Heron]
Ciconiiformes Ardeidae *Egretta caerula*

Far from the Madding Crowd

It seem to me I'd like to go
Where bells don't ring, nor whistles blow,
Nor clocks don't strike, nor gongs sound,
And I'd have stillness all around.

Not real stillness, but just the trees,
Low whispering, or the hum of bees,
Or brooks faint babbling over stones,
In strangely, softly tangled tones.

Or maybe a cricket or katydid,
Or the songs of birds in the hedges hid,
Or just some such sweet sound as these,
To fill a tired heart with ease.

If 'twern't for sight and sound and smell,
I'd like the city pretty well,
But when it comes to getting rest,
I like the country lots the best.

Sometimes it seems to me I must
Just quit the city's din and dust,
And get out where the sky is blue,
And say, now, how does it seem to you?

— Nixon Waterman

PLATE CCLXIX.

Drawn from Nature by J.J.Audubon, F.R.S. F.L.S.

Engraved, Printed & Coloured by R.Havell 1835.

Greenshank.
TOTANUS GLOTTIS, Bechst.
View of St Augustine & Spanish Fort East Florida.

Greenshank
Charadriiformes Scolopacidae *Tringa nebularia*

Sometimes hath the brightest day a cloud;
And after summer evermore succeeds
Barren winter, with his wrathful nipping cold:
So cares and joys abound, as seasons fleet.

—William Shakespeare, *King Henry VI*, Part II, Act 1

PLATE CCCXXVIII

Drawn from Nature by J.J. Audubon, F.R.S. F.L.S.

Engraved, Printed and Coloured by R. Havell. 1836

Long-legged Avocet.
HIMANTOPUS NIGRICOLLIS, *VIEILL.*
Male

Black-necked Stilt [Long-legged Avocet]
Charadriiformes Recurvirostridae *Himantopus mexicanus*

Nature

here are days which occur in this climate, at almost any season of the year, wherein the world reaches perfection, when the air, the heavenly bodies, and the earth make a harmony, as if nature would indulge her offspring—when everything that has life gives sign of satisfaction, and the cattle that lie on the ground seem to have great and tranquil thoughts. These halcyons may be looked for with a little more assurance in that pure October weather, which we distinguish by the name of the Indian Summer. The day, immeasurably long, sleeps over the broad hills and warm wide fields. To have lived through all its sunny hours, seems longevity enough.

—Ralph Waldo Emerson, *Essays*

Summer or Wood Duck.

Wood Duck [Summer or Wood Duck]
Anseriformes Anatidae *Aix sponsa*

To a Skylark

Hail to thee, blithe spirit!
Bird thou never wert—
That from heaven or near it
Pourest thy full heart
In profuse strains of unpremeditated art.

Higher still and higher
From the earth thou springest,
Like a cloud of fire;
The blue deep thou wingest,
And singing still dost soar, and soaring ever singest.

—Percy Bysshe Shelley

White-breasted Black-capped Nuthatch SITTA CAROLINENSIS *Male & Female*

White-breasted Nuthatch [White-breasted Black-capped Nuthatch]
Passeriformes Sittidae *Sitta carolinensis*

Woodpecker and sparrow,
With froggy and gnat,
Attacking *en masse*, laid
The elephant flat.

—The Panchatantra (circa 200 BC)

Night Heron or Qua bird.
ARDEA NYCTICORAX. L.

Black-crowned Night-Heron [Night Heron or Qua bird]
Ciconiiformes Ardeidae *Nycticorax nycticorax*

(Poem on my bedroom wall when I was a child)

I wisht I was a little rock, a sittin' on a hill—
Doin' nothin' all day long, but
Just a sittin' still.
I wouldn't eat; I wouldn't sleep;
I wouldn't even wash.
I'd jus' sit still a thousand years
And rest myself, b'gosh!

—John Borneman, *Memories of J.B.*

Drawn from Nature, by J.J.Audubon. F.R.S. F.L.S.

Engraved, Printed, & Coloured by R. Havell. London. 1833.

Tufted Puffin.
MORMON CIRRHATUS, Lath. *Male 1. Female 2.*

Tufted Puffin [Tufted Auk]
Charadriiformes Alcidae *Fratercula cirrhata*

Nature

It seems as if the day was not wholly profane, in which we have given heed to some natural object. The fall of snowflakes in a still air, preserving to each crystal its perfect form; the blowing of sleet over a wide sheet of water, and over plains, the waving rye-field, the mimic waving action of houstonia, whose innumerable florets whiten and ripple before the eye; the reflections of trees and flowers in glassy lakes; the musical steaming odorous south wind, which converts all trees to windharps; the crackling and spurting of hemlock in the flames; or of pine logs, which yield glory to the walls and faces in the sitting room — these are the music and pictures of the most ancient religion.

—Ralph Waldo Emerson, *Essays*

PLATE CCC

Red-breasted Merganser
MERGUS SERRATOR, *L*
Male 1. Female 2.
Iris arundinacea, Nutt.

Red-breasted Merganser
Anseriformes Anatidae *Mergus serrator*

Pied Beauty

Glory be to God for dappled things—
For skys of couple-colour as a brindled cow;
For rose-moles all in stipple upon trout that swim;
Fresh-firecoal chestnut-falls; finches wings;
Landscape plotted and pieced—fold, fallow, and plough;
and áll trádes, their gear and tackle trim.
All things counter, original, spare, strange;
Whatever is fickle, freckled (who knows how?)
With swift, slow; sweet, sour; adazzle, dim;
He fathers-forth whose beauty is past change:
Praise him.

—Gerard Manley Hopkins

Purple Finch
FRINGILLA PURPUREA ,Gmel,
Male.1,2, Female, 3.
Red Finch — Larix americana

Drawn from nature by J.J.Audubon,F,R,S,F,L,S.   Engraved, Printed & Coloured, by R. Havell, Jun.

Purple Finch
Passeriformes Fringillidae *Carpodacus purpureus*

One night after a thunderstorm over the North Rim, while the stars were still hidden, the moon gave a soft light through which the large landscape features could be discerned. . . . But I gazed around dreamily, the soft, soothing voices of the little toads, the chirring of crickets, and the faint distant poor-will, poor-will* soon lulled me into peaceful sleep.

—Florence Merriam Bailey, *Among the Birds in the Grand Canyon*

*The poor-will is a nocturnal bird of the West, related to the whip-poor-will of the Eastern United States and derives its name from its call.

PLATE LXXXII

Whip-poor-will. CAPRIMULGUS VOCIFERUS. *Male.1.Female. 2.3. Black Oak or Quercitron. Quercus tinctoria.*

Whip-poor-will
Caprimulgiformes Caprimulgidae *Caprimulgus vociferus*

Queen Mab

Oh! not the visioned poet in his dreams,
When silvery clouds float through the wildered brain,
When every sight of lovely, wild and grand
Astonishes, enraptures, elevates,
When fancy at a glance combines
The wondrous and the beautiful,—
So bright, so fair, so wild a shape
Hath ever yet beheld,
As that which reined the coursers of the air
And poured the magic of her gaze
Upon the maiden's sleep.

—Percy Bysshe Shelley

Black Skimmer or Shearwater
RHINCOPS NIGRA. L.
Male.

Black Skimmer [Black Skimmer or Shearwater]
Charadriiformes Rynchopidae *Rynchops niger*

ept. 24, 1870. First saw the Northern Lights. My eye was caught by beams of light and dark very like the crown of horny rays the sun makes behind a cloud. At first I thought of silvery cloud until I saw that these were more luminous and did not dim the clearness of the stars in the Bear. They rose slightly radiating thrown out from the earthline. Then I saw soft pulses of light one after another rise and pass upward arched in shape but waveringly and with the arch broken. They seemed to float, not following the warp of the sphere as falling stars look to do but free though concentrical with it. This busy working of nature wholly independent of the earth and seeming to go on in a strain of time not reckoned by our reckoning of days and years but simpler and as if correcting the preoccupation of the world by being preoccupied with and appealing to and dated to the day of judgement was like a new witness to God and filled me with delightful fear.

—Gerard Manley Hopkins, *The Journal*

Great Auk
Charadriiformes Alcidae *Pinguinus impennis*

The innocent moon, which nothing does but shine,
Moves all the laboring surges of the world.

—Francis Thompson, "Sister Songs, Part II"

Black-throated Guillemot.
MERGULUS ANTIQUUS, Bonap.

Nobbed-billed Auk.
PHALERIS NODIROSTRIS, Bonap.

Curled-Crested Auk.
PHALERIS SUPERCILIATA, Bonap.

Horned-billed Guillemot.
CERATORRHINA OCCIDENTALIS, Bonap.

Ancient
Murrelet
[Black-throated
Guillemot]
Charadriiformes
Alcidae
*Synthliboramphus
antiquus*

Marbled
Murrelet
[Black-throated
Guillemot]
Charadriiformes
Alcidae
*Brachyramphus
marmoratus*

Least Auklet
[Nobbed-billed
Phaleris]
Charadriiformes
Alcidae
Aethia pusilla

Crested Auklet
[Curled-crested
Phaleris]
Charadriiformes
Alcidae
Aethia cristatella

Rhinoceros
Auklet
[Horned-billed
Guillemot]
Charadriiformes
Alcidae
*Cerorhinca
monocereta*

My Piney Wood

I have a tiny piney wood;
My trees are only fifty,
Yet give me shade and solitude
For they are thick and thrifty.
And every day to me they fling
With largess undenying,
Fat cones to make my kettle sing
And keep my pan a-frying.
Go buy yourself a piney wood
If you have gold for spending,
Where you can dream a mellow mood
With peace and joy unending;
Where you can cheerfully retreat
Beyond all churchly chiding,
And make yourself a temple sweet
Of rapturous abiding.

Oh Silence has a secret voice
That claims the soul for portal,
And those who hear it may rejoice
Since they are more than mortal.
So sitting in my piney wood
Where soft the owl is winging,
As still as Druid stone I brood . . .
For hark! the stars are singing.

—Robert W. Service, *Garden Glees*

Blue Jay.
CORVUS CRISTATUS,
Male. 1. Female. 2. 3.

Drawn from nature by J.J. Audubon F.R.S. F.L.S.

Engraved, printed & Coloured by R.Havell

Blue Jay
Passeriformes Corvidae *Cyanocitta cristata*

*T*he Willow-Wren was twittering his thin little song, hidden himself in the dark selvedge of the river bank. Though it was past ten o'clock at night, the sky clung to and retained some lingering skirts of light from the departed day; and the sullen heats of the torrid afternoon broke up and rolled away at the dispersing touch of the cool fingers of the short midsummer night.

—Kenneth Grahame, *The Wind in the Willows*

Great Carolina Wren.
TROGLODYTES LUDOVICIANUS, Bonn. 1 M & 2 Female.
Dwarf Buck-eye. Æsculus Pavia.

Carolina Wren [Great Carolina Wren]
Passeriformes Troglodytidae *Thryothorus ludovicianus*

Song of the Brook

I come from haunts of coot and hern:
I make a sudden sally
And sparkle out among the fern,
To bicker down a valley.

By thirty hills I hurry down,
Or slip between the ridges,
By twenty thorps, a little town,
And half a hundred bridges.

Till last by Phillip's farm I flow
To join the brimming river,
For men may come and men may go,
But I go on forever.

—Alfred, Lord Tennyson

Great blue Heron. ARDEA HERODIAS.

Great Blue Heron
Ciconiiformes Ardeidae *Ardea herodias*

A Song from Sylvan

The little cares that fretted me,
I lost them yesterday
Among the fields above the sea,
Among the winds that play;
Among the lowing herds,
The rustling of the trees,
Among the singing of the birds,
The humming of the bees.

The fears of what may come to pass,
I cast them all away,
Among the clover-scented grass,
Among the new-mown hay;
Among the husking of the corn,
Where the drowsy poppies nod,
Where ill thoughts die and good are born,
Out in the fields with God.

—Louise Imogen Guiney

Yellow Red-poll Warbler
SYLVIA PETECHIA, Lath.
Male 1 & made 2.
Helianthus quindenticitis.

Drawn from Nature by J.J. Audubon FRS. FLS.   Engraved, Printed & Coloured by R. Havell, London, 1832.

Palm Warbler [Yellow Red-poll Warbler]
Passeriformes Parulidae *Dendroica palmarum*

A Woodpecker Musing

*I*t happened on an Audubon Safari Workshop to Kenya and Tanzania in 1974. We had just finished lunch and I was sitting outside of my tent at Ndutu Camp at the edge of the Serengeti Plains. Most of the tourists were napping but my friend, the late Ed Brigham, was polishing his shoes.

A pair of giraffes were ambling among the thorn trees. It is always a strange experience to see animals in their native habitats that one has previously only observed in zoos. So far we had seen elephant, cheetah, lion, rhinoceros, leopard and most of the "sexy" species shown on TV nature shows.

Presently, an African Gray Woodpecker landed on the top of a dead snag next to our tent. Following the usual reaction of "Ah! That's a new one for my life list!" I soon found myself watching it as I have watched downy or hairy woodpeckers at home. It was just doing its woodpecker "thing": chipping pieces of rotting wood off the snag and looking for insects or larvae. It took on the aura of a "familiar" rather than "exotic" creature and when that happened I began to view my surroundings in a different way: The excitement of being in Africa was replaced by a feeling of contentment such as one experiences in one's own chair in one's home . . . I could relax! I could even watch the giraffes without feeling the compulsion to grab my binoculars!

Ed continued to polish his shoes, the giraffes continued to munch on the thorn trees, the woodpecker continued to chip away on the snag and I fell asleep in my chair under the warm, equatorial sun.

—John Borneman, *Memories of J.B.*

Hairy Woodpecker [Maria's Phillips's, Canadian,
Harris's and Audubon's Woodpeckers]
Piciformes Picidae *Picoides villosus*

Three-toed Woodpecker
[Banded Three-toed Woodpecker]
Piciformes Picidae *Picoides tridactylus*

Summer Moods

I love at eventide to walk alone,
Down narrow glens, o'erhung with dewy thorn,
Where, from the long grass underneath, the snail,
Jet black, creeps out, and sprouts his timid horn.
I love to muse o'er meadows newly mown,
Where bees search round, with sad and weary drone,
In vain, for flowers that bloomed but newly there;
While in the juicy corn the hidden quail
Cries, "Wet my foot"; and, hid as thoughts unborn,
The fairy-like and seldom seen land-rail
Utters "Craik, craik," like voices underground,
Right glad to meet the evening's dewy veil,
And see the light fade into gloom around.

—John Clare

PLATE CCXXVIII

Drawn from Nature by J. J. Audubon, F.R.S. F.L.S.

Great Marbled Godwit. 1 Male. 2 Female.
LIMOSA FEDOA. Vieill.

Engraved, Printed, & Coloured, by R. Havell. London 1834

Marbled Godwit [Great Marbled Godwit]
Charadriiformes Scolopacidae *Limosa fedoa*

Beauty Is All

Beauty is in the eye and mind,
And as we stand and stare,
The more we seek the more we find
Of Beauty everywhere.
Day-long it woos from hill and dale,
From woods and meadow bars,
Until in holy night we hail
The beauty of the stars.

Today for long I stood alone
And watched beside a brook,
A silver rill that leapt a stone
And spray of jewels shook.
Drowned sunbeams graved the gravel gold,
And dream-enraptured there,
I thought: Lo! here is wealth untold
To make me millionaire!

Oh, Beauty stab me wide awake
To see with quickened eyes;
And through the magic lens of air
Behold enchanted skies!
Aye, though a vagabond I be,
My lot of daily dearth,
With wand of wonder make of me
The richest man on earth!

—Robert W. Service, *Rhymes for a Recluse*

PLATE. CCLXVIII

American Woodcock.
SCOLOPAX MINOR, Gmel.
Male 1. Female 2. Young Autumn 3.

Drawn from Nature by J.J. Audubon, F.R.S. F.L.S.

Engraved, Printed & coloured, by R. Havell, London, 1835.

American Woodcock
Charadriiformes Scolopacidae *Scolopax minor*

Just So Stories

... There was never a king like Solomon,
Not since the world began;
But Solomon talked to a butterfly
As a man would talk to a man.

—Rudyard Kipling

Arkansaw Flycatcher.
MUSCICAPA VERTICALIS, *Bonap.*
1. Male. 2. Female.
Drawn from Nature by J.J. Audubon, F.R.S. F.L.S.

Swallow-Tailed Flycatcher.
MUSCICAPA FORFICATA, *Gm.*
3. Male.

Says Flycatcher.
MUSCICAPA SAYA, *Bonap.*
4.Male. 5.Female.
Engraved, Printed and Coloured by R. Havell 1837.

Western Kingbird
[Arkansaw Flycatcher]
Passeriformes Tyrannidae
Tyrannus verticalis

Scissor-tailed Flycatcher
[Swallow-tailed Flycatcher]
Passeriformes Tyrannidae
Tyrannus forficatus

Say's Phoebe
Say's Flycatcher]
Passeriformes Tyrannidae
Sayornis saya

Out of Film

*I*t was in Tsavo Park, Tanzania, when I ran out of film. We had been rushing around Kenya and Tanzania, seeing lions, cheetahs, elephants, ground hornbills and a myriad of species. Folks were climbing into the vans for another long day to see more and more wonders. Now, I'm normally quite an extrovert, but frankly I was "peopled out"! I opted to stay at the lodge.

I found a spot in the shade overlooking the savanna that hosted a scattering of baobab trees. It was still — I didn't even have to listen to my own voice, cracking puns, pointing out birds and answering "I don't know" when I couldn't think up a plausible answer to a question.

For two weeks I had seen East Africa through the lens of a camera, but today I could just sit, listen, smell and absorb. It was a wonderful day.

—John Borneman, *Memories of J.B.*

American Flamingo.
PHOENICOPTERUS RUBER. Linn.
Old Male.

Greater Flamingo
Phoenicopteriformes Phoenicopteridae *Phoenicopterus ruber*

Thoughts fer the Discuraged Farmer

Does the medder-lark complane, as he swims high and dry
Through the waves of the wind and the blue of the sky?
Does the quail set up and whissel in a disappointed way,
Er hang his head in silunce, and sorrow all the day?

Is the chipmuck's health a-failin'? — Does he walk, er does he run?
Don't the buzzards ooze around up thare jest like they've allus done?
Is they anything the matter with the rooster's lungs er voice?
Ort a mortul be complanin' when dumb animals rejoice?

Then let us, one and all, be contented with our lot;
The June is here this mornin', and the sun is shining hot . . .
Fer the world is full of roses, and the roses full of dew,
And the dew is full of heavenly love that drips fer me and you.

—James Whitcomb Riley

Shore Lark.

ALAUDA ALPESTRIS.:

Male adult Summer plumage. 1 & 2 Male Winter plumage; 3 Young & 5 6

Horned Lark [Shore Lark]
Passeriformes Alaudidae *Eremophila alpestris*

It is spring, and the fresh grass is sprinkled with buttercups and spring-beauties. How divine are the violets! Or the phlox fills the spaces with a misty flush.

June! O love and roses and fullness of life!—can we ask any more? Kind Heaven, how good to all creation! Let us lie full-length, with faces in the grass, and hear the stream ripple and sing over its rocky be.

—Katharine Dooris Sharp, *Summer in a Bog*

Drawn from Nature by J.J.Audubon, F.R.S. F.L.S.

Engraved, Printed and Coloured by R. Havell 1837.

Lazuli Finch.
FRINGILLA AMOENA,
1. Male Spring Plumage

Clay-Coloured Finch.
EMBERIZA PALLIDA, *Swains.*
2. Male.
Plant-Liberty Bush.
AZALEA NUDIFLORA,

Oregon Snow Finch.
FRINGILLA OREGONA, *Towns*
3. Male & Female.

Lazuli Bunting
[Lazuli Finch]
Passeriformes Emberizidae
Passerina amoena

Dark-eyed Junco
[Oregon Snow Finch]
Passeriformes Emberizidae
Junco hyemalis

Clay-colored Sparrow
[Clay-coloured Finch]
Passeriformes Emberizidae
Spizella pallida

I Saw God Wash the World

I saw God wash the world last night
With his sweet showers on high,
And then when morning came, I saw
Him hang it out to dry.

He washed each tiny blade of grass
And every trembling tree;
He flung his showers against the hill,
And swept the billowing sea.

The white rose is a cleaner white,
The red rose is more red,
Since God washed every fragrant face
And put them all to bed.
There's not a bird, there's not a bee
That wings along the way
But is a cleaner bird and bee
Than it was yesterday.

I saw God wash the world last night.
Ah, would He had washed me
As clean of all my dust and dirt
As that old white birch tree.

—William L. Stidger

Long-billed Curlew. NUMENIUS AMERICANUS. *1 Male. 2 Female. Mew of Charleston.*

Long-billed Curlew
Charadriiformes Scolopacidae *Numenius americanus*

If the Father deigns to touch with
divine power the cold and pulseless
heart of the buried acorn and to make
it burst forth from its prison walls, will
He leave neglected in the earth the soul
of man made in the image of his Creator?

—William Jennings Bryan, Speech at the
National Democratic Convention, Chicago, 1896

PLATE LXVII

Red-winged Starling or Marsh Blackbird.
ICTERUS PHŒNICEUS, Daud.
Adult Male, 1.Young Male 2.Female Old 3.Young 4.
Red Maple or Swamp Maple, Acer rubrum.

Red-winged Blackbird [Red-winged Starling]
Passeriformes Icteridae *Aglelaius phoeniceus*

Long-billed Marsh Wren

When woods and fields have lost their relish, spend a day in a marsh and the world will seem young again. The expanse of the great level stretch, 'its range and its sweep'—a dark green sea interrupted only by its narrow winding river, seemingly bounded only by the horizon where treetops meet the small round clouds bordering the soft June heavens—both the expanse and solitude of the great green plain under the sky are infinitely restful.

But, aside from this, the marsh is a little world apart, offering keen, peculiar pleasures to those who know nature only in her more familiar forms. As you wade through the reeds, the long blades make pleasant music in your ears, seething as they bow before you and rise behind you. . . . As for birds, they pervade the margins of the plain and give it life. At one moment you are remonstrated with by Maryland Yellow-throats, small yellow birds who whip in and out of the reeds, peering up at you anxiously to make out if you would really harm their brood.

—Florence Merriam Bailey, *Birds of Village and Field*

PLATE CCX

Least Bittern. ARDEA EXILIS. ca. 1. Male 2. Female 3. Young.

Least Bittern
Ciconiiformes Ardeidae *Ixobrychus exilis*

Is it by your wisdom that the hawk soars,
and spreads its wings toward the south?

Is it at your command that the eagle mounts up
and makes its nest on high?
It lives on the rock and makes its home
in the fastness of the rocky crag.

—Job 39:26–28

Stanley Hawk

Cooper's Hawk [Stanley Hawk]
Falconiformes Accipitridae *Accipiter cooperii*

Brute Neighbors

It is remarkable how many creatures live wild and free though secret in the woods, and still sustain themselves in the neighborhood of towns. . . .You need only to sit long enough in some attractive spot in the woods that all its inhabitants may exhibit themselves to you by turns.

—Henry David Thoreau, *Walden*

Ruby-throated Humming Bird.

TROCHILUS COLUBRIS, *Linn.*

Male, 1. Female, 2. Young, 3.

Trumpet flower. Bignonia radicans.

Engraved, Printed & Coloured by R. Havell.

Drawn from Nature and Published by John J. Audubon, F.R.S.F.L.S.

Ruby-throated Hummingbird [Ruby-throated Humming Bird]
Apodiformes Trochilidae *Archilochus colubris*

The Swing

How do you like to go up in a swing,
Up in the air so blue?
Oh, I do think it the pleasantest thing
Ever a child can do!

Up in the air and over the wall,
Till I can see so wide,
Rivers and trees and cattle and all
Over the countryside—

Till I look down on the garden green,
Down on the roof so brown—
Up in the air I go flying again,
Up in the air and down!

—Robert Lewis Stevenson, *A Child's Garden of Verses*

PLATE CCCXIII

Drawn from Nature by J. J. Audubon, F.R.S. F.L.S.

Engraved, Printed, & Coloured by R. Havell 1836

Blue-Winged Teal.
ANAS DISCORS, L.
Male 1, Female 2.

Blue-winged Teal
Anseriformes Anatidae *Anas discors*

The Seasons of Sound

Early Spring: Peepers in ponds and puddles.
Late Spring: Whispers of warblers.
Early Summer: Melodic mating music of mockingbirds.
Midsummer: Booming of bullfrogs in backwaters.
Late Summer: Cacophony of calling cicadas.
Early Autumn: Crisp, incessant, creaking of katydids.
Late Autumn: Cries of columns of Canada geese.
Early Winter: Whistling winds.
Late Winter: Hollow hootings of horned owls.

—John Borneman, *Memories of J.B.*

PLATE CCCXXVII

Shoveller Duck.
ANAS CLYPEATA. *L.*

Northern Shoveler [Shoveller Duck]
Anseriformes Anatidae *Anas clypeata*

The Wild Swans at Coole

The trees are in their autumn
    beauty,
The woodland paths are dry,
Under the October twilight the
    water
Mirrors the still sky;
Upon the brimming water among
    the stones
Are nine and fifty swans.

The nineteenth autumn has come
    upon me
Since I first made my count;
I saw, before I had well finished,
All suddenly mount
And scatter wheeling in great
    broken rings
Upon their clamorous wings.

I have looked upon those brilliant
    creatures,
And now my heart is sore.
All's changed since I, hearing at
    twilight,

The first time on this shore,
The bell-beat of their wings
    above my head,
Trod with a lighter tread.

Unwearied still, lover by lover,
They paddle in the cold
Companionable streams or climb
    the air;
Their hearts have not grown old;
Passion or conquest, wander
    where they will,
Attend upon them still.

But now they drift on the still
    water,
Mysterious, beautiful;
Among what rushes will they
    build,
By what lake's edge or pool
Delight men's eyes when I awake
    some day
To find they have flown away?

—William Butler Yeats

PLATE CCCCXI

Common American Swan.
CYGNUS AMERICANUS, Sharpless
Nymphaea Flava - Nuttall

Tundra Swan [Common American Swan]
Anseriformes Anatidae *Cygnus columbianus*

Camping on the Tejon Ranch

It was mid October, the time of the annual "Condor Survey." The last three condors had dropped into the safety of tree-filled House Canyon, where they would preen, change positions, spar for roosting sites and settle in for the night.

As the night closed in on the honey-colored, dry slopes of the Tejon, cool breezes carried the fragrance of dry, moist straw down the slopes and the great horned owls began hooting back and forth between the ridges. The 100° day had cooled rapidly and the night was coming alive with the nocturnal creatures that had remained unseen throughout the day. A campfire was lit (making sure the ground was cleared around its location) and food and drink was prepared, poured, eaten and drunk with much enthusiasm after a long day's vigil on a blistering ridge top.

As the fire began to grow dim, the chill, down-slope breeze encouraged us to seek the comfort of sleeping bags, where, with heads cradled on crossed hands, eyes focused on the home of the Pleiades, Orion, the Dippers, the Milky Way and "The Heavenly Host." An occasional meteorite would leave a trail and a tumbling man-made satellite would make its way across the sky.

The only sounds were the soughing of the wind through the pines on the ridge tops, the dry flapping of oak leaves and perhaps a chorus of coyotes. The last sound to be heard before drifting off to sleep might be the "schreech" of a barn owl or the piping of a screech owl.

—John Borneman, *Memories of J.B.*

Eastern Screech-Owl [Mottled Owl]
Strigiformes Strigidae *Otus asio*

When the Frost Is on the Punkin

When the frost is on the punkin and the fodders in the shock,
And you hear the kyouck and gobble of the struttin' turkey cock,
And the clackin' of the guineys, and the cluckin' of the hens,
And the rooster's hallylooer as he tiptoes on the fence;
O, it's then's the time a feller is a-feelin' at his best,
With the risen' sun to greet him from a night of peaceful rest,
As he leaves the house, bare-headed, and goes out to feed the stock,
When the frost is on the punkin and the fodder's on the shock.

They's something kindo' hearty-like about the atmusfere
When the heat of summer's over and the coolin' fall is here —
Of course we miss the flowers, and the blossums on the trees,
And the mumble of the hummin'-birds and the buzzin' of the bees;
But the air's so appetizin'; and the landscape through the haze
Of a crisp and sunny morning of the airly autumn days
Is a pictur' that no painter has the colorin' to mock —
When the frost is on the punkin and the fodder's in the shock!

—James Whitcomb Riley

Wild Turkey [Great American Hen]
Galliformes Phasianidae *Meleagris gallopavo*

The Latter Rain

The latter rain—it falls in anxious haste
Upon the sun-dried fields and branches bare,
Loosening with searching drops the rigid waste
As if it would each root's lost strength repair;
But not a blade grows green as in the Spring;
No swelling twig puts forth its thickening leaves;
The robins only mid the harvests sing,
Pecking the grain that scatters from the sheaves;
The rain falls still—the fruit all ripened drops,
It pierces chestnut-burr and walnut-shell;
The furrowed fields disclose the yellow crops;
Each bursting pod of talents used can tell;
And all that once received the early rain
Declare to man it was not sent in vain.

—Jones Very

PLATE XCVI.

Columbia Jay.

Black-throated Magpie-Jay [Columbia Jay]
Passeriformes Corvidae *Calocitta colliei*

*A*t length the winter set in in good earnest, just as I had finished plastering, and the wind began to howl around the house as if it had not permission to do so till then. Night after night the geese came lumbering in in the dark with a clangor and whistling of wings, even after the ground was covered with snow, some to alight in Walden, and some flying low over the woods toward Fair Haven, bound for Mexico.

—Henry David Thoreau, *Walden*

PLATE CCCLXXI

Snow Goose
ANSER HYPERBOREUS, *Pallas*

Snow Goose
Anseriformes Anatidae *Chen caerulescens*

Daffodils

I wandered lonely as a cloud
That floats on high o'er vales and hills,
When all at once I saw a crowd—
A host of golden daffodils
Beside the lake, beneath the trees,
Fluttering and dancing in the breeze.

Continuous as the stars that shine
And twinkle on the Milky Way,
They stretched in never-ending line
Along the margin of the bay:
Ten thousand saw I, at a glance,
Tossing their heads in spritely dance.

The waves beside them danced, but they
Outdid the sparkling waves in glee;
A poet could not but be gay
In such a jocund company;
I gazed—and gazed—but little thought
What wealth the show to me had brought.

For oft, when on my couch I lie,
In vacant or in pensive mood,
They flash upon that inward eye
Which is the bliss of solitude;
And then my heart with pleasure fills,
And dances with the daffodils.

—William Wordsworth

Mallard [Mallard Duck]
Anseriformes Anatidae *Anas platyrhynchos*

Spring

he first sparrow of spring! The year beginning with younger hope than ever! The faint silvery warblings heard over the partially bare and moist fields from the bluebirds, the song sparrow, and the red-wing, as if the last flakes of winter tinkled as they fell! What at such times are histories, chronologies, traditions, and all written revelations?

—Henry David Thoreau, *Walden*

Blue-bird.

SYLVIA SIALIS.

Eastern Bluebird [Blue-bird]
Passeriformes Turdidae *Sialia sialis*

When the Green Gits Back in the Trees

In spring, when the green gits back in the trees,
And the sun comes out and stays,
And yer boots pulls on with a good tight squeeze,
And you think of yer barefoot days;
When you ort to work and you want to not,
And you and yer wife agrees
It's time to spade up the garden-lot,
When the green gits back in the trees—
Well! work is the least o' my idees
When the green, you know, gits back in the trees!

—James Whitcomb Riley

PLATE. CLXXXV.

Bachman's Warbler. SYLVIA BACHMANII. Male 1 Female 2. Gordonia pubescens

Bachman's Warbler
Passeriformes Parulidae *Vermivora bachmanii*

S weet flowers grow beside the fallen tree, among shattered branches, the season through; and the freedom of the woods, the unchecked growth, the careless position of every tree, are favorable to a thousand wild beauties, and fantastic forms, opening to the mind a play of fancy which is in itself cheering and enlivening, like the bright sunbeams which checker with golden light the shadowy groves. That character of rich variety also, stamped on all the works of creation, is developed in the forest in clear and noble forms; we are told that in the field we shall not find two blades of grass exactly alike, that in the garden we shall not gather two flowers precisely similar, but in those cases the lines are minute, and we do not seize the truth at once; in the woods, however, the same fact stands recorded in bolder lines; we cannot fail to mark the great variety of detail among the trees; we see it in their trunks, their branches, their foliage; in the rude knots, the gnarled roots; in the mosses and lichens which feed upon their bark; in their forms, their coloring, their shadows. And within all this luxuriance of varied beauty, there dwells a sweet quiet, a noble harmony, a calm repose, which we seek in vain elsewhere, in so full a measure.

—Susan Fenimore Cooper, *Rural Hours*

Baltimore Oriole. ICTERUS BALTIMORE. Bond. *Adult Male,1.Male two years old.2.Female.3 . Tulip - Tree Liriodendron tulipifera*

Drawn from Nature by J.J.Audubon, F.R.S.F.L.S.   Engraved & Printed, & Coloured, by R.Havell

Northern Oriole [Baltimore Oriole]
Passeriformes Icteridae *Icterus galbula*

My Garden

The world is sadly sick, they say,
And plagued by woe and pain.
But look! How looms my garden gay,
With blooms in golden reign!
With lyric music in the air,
Of joy fullfilled in song,
I can't believe that any where
Is hate and harm and wrong.

A paradise my garden is,
And there my day is spent;
I steep myself in sunny bliss,
Incredibly content.
Feeling that I am truly part
Of peace so rapt and still,
There's not a care within my heart . . .
How can the world be ill?

Aye, though the land be sick, they say,
And naked unto pain,
My garden never was so gay,
So innocent, so sane.
My roses mock at misery,
My thrushes vie in song . . .
When only beauty I can see,
How *can* the world be wrong?

—Robert W. Service, *Garden Glees*

PLATE LXXIX

Wood Thrush
TURDUS MUSTELINUS Aud.
Male 1. Female 2.
Dogwood. Cornus florida.

Wood Thrush
Passeriformes Turdidae *Hylocichla mustelina*

*T*he line of the horizon was clear and hard against the sky, and in one particular quarter it showed black against a silvery climbing phosphorescence that grew and grew. At last, over the rim of the waiting earth the moon lifted with slow majesty till it swung clear of the horizon and rode off, free of moorings; and once more they began to see surfaces—meadows widespread, and quiet gardens, and the river itself from bank to bank, all softly disclosed, all washed clean of mystery and terror, all radiant again as by day, but with a difference that was tremendous. Their old haunts greeted them again in other rainment, as if they had slipped away and put on this pure new apparel and come quietly back, smiling as they shyly waited to see if they would be recognized again under it.

—Kenneth Grahame, *The Wind in the Willows*

PLATE CCXVI

Wood Ibis. *TANTALUS LOCULATOR.*

Wood Stork [Wood Ibis]
Ciconiiformes Ciconiidae *Mycteria americana*

The Wind

Of all the sounds dispatched abroad
There's not a charge to me
Like that old measure in the boughs,
That phraseless melody

The wind does, working like a hand
Whose fingers brush the sky,
Then quiver down, with tufts of tune
Permitted gods and me.

When winds go round and round in bands,
And thrum upon the door,
And birds take places overhead,
To bear them orchestra,

I crave him grace, of summer boughs,
If such an outcast be,
He never heard that fleshless chant
Rise solemn in the tree,

As if some caravan of sound
On deserts, in the sky,
Had broken rank,
Then knit, and passed
In seamless company.

—Emily Dickinson

Bohemian Chatterer.
BOMBYCILLA GARRULA.
Male 1. Female 2.
Pyrus Americana canadensis. Service Tree.

Drawn from Nature by J.J. Audubon, F.R.S. F.L.S.　　　　Engraved, Printed and Coloured by R. Havell 1836.

Bohemian Waxwing [Bohemian Chatterer]
Passeriformes Bombycillidae *Bombycilla garrulus*

Even the stork in the heavens
knows its times;
and the turtledove, swallow and crane
observe the time of their coming.

—Jeremiah 8:7

Whooping Crane [Hooping Crane]
Gruiformes Gruidae *Grus americana*

Thankfullness

"God is so good to me," I said,
As with the golden dawn I rose.
"How can poor people lie abed
When all the land with gladness glows?"
Then drinking deep of air like wine,
And listening to winged delight,
And gazing wide with eyes ashine
On beauty that bewitched my sight,
I thanked the Lord who granted me
His gift of lovliness to see.
I give thanks for my daily bread
And appetite to savor it,
The cosy roof above my head,
My body marvellously fit.
I give thanks for the sea and sky,
And stars and trees and linnet wings;
I bless the Lord that I am I,
And part of all the sum of things.
I'm thankful for the boon of breath,
And will be to the door of death.

—Robert W. Service

Arctic Tern.
STERNA ARCTICA.

Arctic Tern
Charadriiformes Laridae *Sterna paradisaea*

Woodman, Spare That Tree

Woodman, spare that tree!
Touch not a single bough!
In youth it sheltered me,
And I'll protect it now.
'Twas my forefather's hand
That placed it near his cot;
There, woodman, let it stand,
Thy axe shall harm it not!

That old familiar tree
Whose glory and renown
Are spread o'er land and sea,
And wouldst thou hew it down?
Woodman, forbear thy stroke!
Cut not its earthbound ties;
O, spare that aged oak,
Now towering to the skies!

When but an idle boy
I sought its grateful shade;
In all their gushing joy
Here too my sisters played.
My mother kissed me here;
My father pressed my hand—
Forgive this foolish tear,
But let that old oak stand!

My heart-strings round thee cling,
Close as thy bark, old friend!
Here shall the wild-bird sing,
And still thy branches bend,
Old tree! the storm still brave!
And woodman, leave the spot;
While I've a hand to save,
Thy axe shall hurt it not.

—George Morris

PLATE LXII

Passenger Pigeon.
COLUMBA MIGRATORIA. *Linn.*
Male 1. Female 2.

Passenger Pigeon
Columbiformes Columbidae *Ectopiste migratorius*

The Woman Botanist

Always a voice is calling
In the city's roar and clangor,
Or the silence of the room;
Now with tender message pleading,
Or, again, with loud insistence
When the world is all abloom.

'Tis the voice of the lone wild-wood,
Of the forests man-forsaken,
Of the meadows flower-gemmed;
Of the streams that murmur softly
O'er the white and shining pebbles,
'Tween the banks with sedges hemmed.

'Tis the voice of Mother Nature,
From her cool and dim recesses,
In the places undefiled.
O, I hunger for the woodland,
And I hear her, and I answer,
And I seek her, I her child!

—Katharine Dooris Sharp

Nuttall's lesser-marsh Wren.
TROGLODYTES BREVIROSTRIS.
Male 1 Female. 2

Sedge Wren [Nuttall's Lesser Marsh Wren]
Passeriformes Troglodytidae *Cistothorus platensis*

About the Editor

John Borneman joined the staff of the National Audubon Society in 1961 as a teacher/naturalist at the Audubon Center of Southern California in El Monte, California. He retired in 1993 after working as Condor Naturalist and Western Regional Representative. He has also led a number of Audubon eco-tours. John was born in Elkhart, Indiana, in 1930. He graduated from the University of Indiana with a degree in Music Education with an opera emphasis. Following a two-year stint in the army, he joined the Fred Waring's Pennsylvanians as a singer/ comedian and was a co-founder of the Dapper Dans of Disneyland barbershop quartet. His interest in spelunking, mountain climbing and natural history and birds, led him to his career with the National Audubon Society. His knowledge of the out-of-doors was gained from personal observation, reading and working closely with biologists and naturalists. He is currently compiling writings on his observations of people and nature. A few of these writings are included in this book as *Memories of J.B.*